**Managing Editor**
Mara Ellen Guckian

**Editor in Chief**
Karen J. Goldfluss, M.S. Ed.

**Creative Director**
Sarah M. Fournier

**Cover Artist**
Diem Pascarella

**Illustrator**
Kelly McMahon

**Art Coordinator**
Renée Mc Elwee

**Imaging**
James Edward Grace
Craig Gunnell

**Publisher**
Mary D. Smith, M.S. Ed.

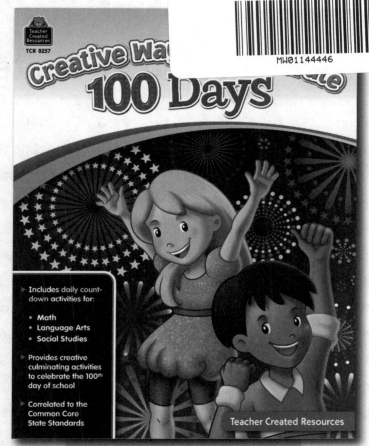

Creative Ways to Celebrate
# 100 Days

Includes daily count-down activities for:
- Math
- Language Arts
- Social Studies

Provides creative culminating activities to celebrate the 100th day of school

Correlated to the Common Core State Standards

Teacher Created Resources

TCR 8257

MW01144446

**Author**
Brenda Shelton Strickland

CORRELATED TO
COMMON CORE
STANDARDS

For correlations to Common Core State Standards, see page 4 of this book or visit *http://teachercreated.com/standards/*.

**Teacher Created Resources**
6421 Industry Way
Westminster, CA 92683
www.teachercreated.com
ISBN: 978-1-4206-8257-1
© 2015 Teacher Created Resources
Made in U.S.A.

Teacher Created Resources

# Table of Contents

# Introduction

The 100th day of school is a day to celebrate. It is an important event for students, but also for the teachers. The 100th day of school is a perfect time to reflect on what has been learned, and to look forward to how much more learning will be done as the school year continues. This is a day that Pre K–Grade 2 students can have fun with the number 100 and share the language arts, math, art, social studies, and physical-education skills they have been developing. It is also a day to share special projects and perhaps a surprise or two!

*Creative Ways to Celebrate 100 Days* provides ideas and activities to showcase the number 100 and what it means. You will find cross-curricular ideas to implement the day or week that school begins. Some of the suggested activities will culminate on the 100th day, and others will continue to the end of the year. Establishing these activities in the beginning is well worth the effort.

Other suggested activities do not need to start at the beginning of the school year. These activities can be embedded into your math, language arts, social studies, and physical-education curricula at any time. Templates are provided throughout to be used for specific activities and /or combined to create a *100 Days Memory Book.*

A special section is devoted to ideas to commemorate and celebrate the 100th day of school.

Suggestions are also provided for activities to finish the school year.

# Common Core State Standards

Each lesson and activity meets one or more of the following Common Core State Standards © Copyright 2010. National Governors Association Center for Best Practices and Council of Chief State School Officers. All rights reserved. For more information about the Common Core State Standards, go to *http://www.corestandards.org/* or *http://www.teachercreated.com/standards/*.

| Math–Kindergarten | Pages |
|---|---|
| **MATH. K.CC.A.1** Count to 100 by ones and by tens. | 5–10, 14, 16–22, 25–27, 30–33, 43–45, 53–56 |
| **MATH. K.CC.A.2** Count forward beginning from a given number within the known sequence (instead of having to begin at 1). | 5–10, 14, 16–21, 25–39, 45 |
| **MATH. K.CC.A.3** Write numbers from 0 to 20. Represent a number of objects with a written numeral 0-20 (with 0 representing a count of no objects). | 5–7, 18–19 |
| **MATH. K.CC.B.4** Understand the relationship between numbers and quantities; connect counting to cardinality. | 5–9, 14–19, 22, 25–27, 33–38, 43–46, 53–56 |
| **MATH. K.CC.B.5** Count to answer "how many?" questions about as many as 20 things arranged in a line, a rectangular array, or a circle, or as many as 10 things in a scattered configuration; given a number from 1-20, count out that many objects. | 5–7, 14, 18, 33–39, 45 |
| **MATH. K.CC.C.6** Identify whether the number of objects in one group is greater than, less than, or equal to the number of objects in another group, e.g., by using matching and counting strategies.[1] (Include groups with up to 10 objects.) | 5–7, 16, 33–37 |
| **Math. K.CC.C.7** Compare two numbers between 1 and 10 presented as written numerals. | 5 |
| **MATH.K.MD.A.1** Describe measurable attributes of objects, such as length or weight. Describe several measurable attributes of a single object. | 27, 29–32 |
| **MATH.K.MD.B.3** Classify objects into given categories; count the numbers of objects in each category and sort categories by count. | 34–37 |
| **Math–First Grade** | |
| **MATH.1.NBT.A.1** Count to 120, starting at any number less than 120. In this range, read and write numerals and represent a number of objects with a written numeral. | 5–9, 14, 16–22, 24–39, 43, 53–54 |
| **MATH.1.NBT.B.2** Understand that the two digits of a two-digit number represent amounts of tens and ones. Understand the following as special cases: | 5–9, 17–33, 53–55, 58–64 |
| **MATH.1.NBT.B.2.A** 10 can be thought of as a bundle of ten ones—called a "ten." | 6–7, 18, 25–27, 53 |
| **MATH.1.MD.A.2** Express the length of an object as a whole number of length units, by laying multiple copies of a shorter object (the length unit) end to end; understand that the length measurement of an object is the number of same-size length units that span it with no gaps or overlaps. | 27, 29 |
| **Math–Second Grade** | |
| **MATH.2.NBT.A.1.A** 100 can be thought of as a bundle of ten tens — called a "hundred." | 6–7, 18 |
| **MATH.2.MD.A.1** Measure the length of an object by selecting and using appropriate tools such as rulers, yardsticks, meter sticks, and measuring tapes. | 27, 29–30 |
| **MATH.2.MD.A.3** Estimate lengths using units of inches, feet, centimeters, and meters. | 29–30 |
| **Reading–Kindergarten** | |
| **ELA.SL.K.2** Confirm understanding of a text read aloud or information presented orally or through other media by asking and answering questions about key details and requesting clarification if something is not understood. | 5–6, 38, 40, 50 |
| **ELA.L.K.1** Demonstrate command of the conventions of standard English grammar and usage when writing or speaking. | 11–15, 40, 45, 50 |
| **ELA.L.K.2** Demonstrate command of the conventions of standard English capitalization, punctuation, and spelling when writing. | 11–12, 40–43, 45 |
| **Reading–First Grade** | |
| **ELA.SL.1.2** Ask and answer questions about key details in a text read aloud or information presented orally or through other media. | 5–6, 38, 50 |
| **ELA.L.1.1** Demonstrate command of the conventions of standard English grammar and usage when writing or speaking. | 11–15, 40, 45, 50 |
| **ELA.L.1.2** Demonstrate command of the conventions of standard English capitalization, punctuation, and spelling when writing. | 11–12, 40–43, 45 |
| **Reading–Second Grade** | |
| **ELA.L.2.1** Demonstrate command of the conventions of standard English grammar and usage when writing or speaking. | 11–15, 40, 45 |
| **ELA.L.2.2** Demonstrate command of the conventions of standard English capitalization, punctuation, and spelling when writing. | 11–12, 40–43, 45 |

# 100 Days Count-Off—Start Now!

## Materials

☐ Class Calendar       ☐ 100s Chart (see p.21)

## Directions

1. Each day, start with the number 1 and count up to the current day's number on a calendar. This may seem repetitive, but it is a great way to reinforce counting skills and later, to develop patterns.

2. Then mark the next number off on the 100s chart you are using to count down to 100 days.

3. Discuss each number you mark on the 100s chart. Students may not understand at first, but they will start to pick up on the different math and language arts concepts you are addressing. Depending on the age of your students, you might focus on one of the following ideas:

   - Does the number have straight lines, curves, or both?
   - Does the number have one digit, or two?
   - Is the number odd or even?
   - Is the number someone's age or birthdate number in our class?
   - Is the number special for some other reason?

4. As skills develop and the number on the 100s chart increases, ask more questions.

   - Is the number a multiple of 2, 5, or 10? If so, count again by that multiple.
   - Is the number *greater than* or *less than* _____?

5. Discuss patterns you create on the 100s chart.

   - Where are the even numbers and the odd numbers?
   - Where are the multiples of 2, 5, and 10?
   - Are there other patterns?

# Counting Sticks

Establish a means of counting objects to keep track of the number of days. Do this in conjunction with "calendar time" or the morning meeting, when the whole class is together.

## Materials

☐ 100 craft sticks or straws
☐ pipe cleaners or rubber bands
☐ 3 cans, envelopes, or small boxes labeled **Ones**, **Tens**, and **Hundreds**

## Directions

1. Keep the sticks in a container near the whole group meeting area. Explain that one stick will be counted for each day of school and added to the container labeled **Ones**.

2. Continue adding a stick for each day and counting the total. When you get to 10, bundle the group of ten using a rubber band. Place the whole bundle in the **Tens** container.

3. Once the day's stick has been added, count the totals. How many ones? How many groups of ten? Discuss the totals using math facts terms. *We have two bundles of 10 plus 4 ones.*

4. Write each new number in the air or on a small piece of paper.

5. Enthusiasm should build as the bundles of ten grow and Celebration Day nears.

# A 100 Days Counting Jar

Keep track of the number of days with a 100 Days Counting Jar. Do this in conjunction with "calendar time." Once initiated, make certain it is done each day to build enthusiasm.

## Materials

☐ large, clear plastic container with lid
☐ collection of 100 items that will eventually fit in the container such as marbles, jacks, small erasers, plastic bugs, or a random collection of items

## Directions

1. Attach the label below to the container.

2. Each day, add an object from the collection to the 100 Days Counting Jar.

3. Occasionally, allow students to dump out the items in the jar and count them. Write the number of items on a small piece of paper or sticky note and stick it to the back of the jar.

4. As time passes and more items are in the container, students can arrange the items in groups and count by 2s, 5s, or 10s.

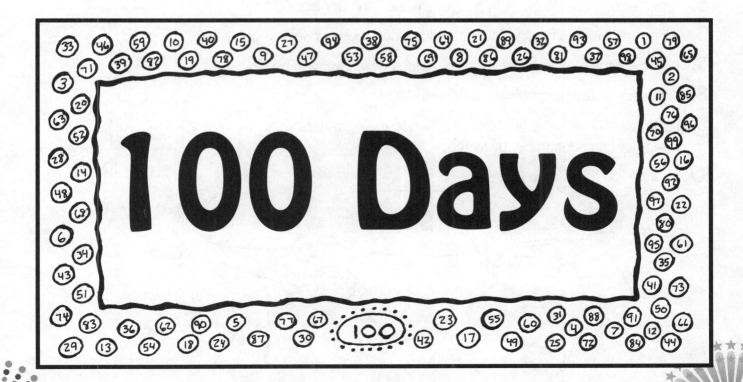

# 10 Physical Education Activities

## Optional Materials

☐ balls          ☐ chalk          ☐ hula hoops          ☐ jump ropes

## Movement Activities

1. Stretch!  Here are some ideas to get you started:
   - Alternate leaning to the left 5 times and then leaning to the right 5 times.
   - Alternate leaning backwards 5 times and leaning forward 5 times (reaching toward toes).
   - Do 5 neck rolls to the left and 5 neck rolls to the right.

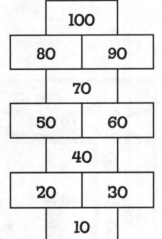

2. Do different exercises adding up to 100.  Try the suggestions below, or substitute other student favorites:
   - 20 arm circles
   - 20 jumping jacks
   - 20 hops on two feet
   - 20 hops—10 on left foot and then 10 on right foot
   - 20 steps—running in place.  Focus on keeping knees up!

3. Work with a partner to bounce a ball 100 times.

4. Jump rope 100 times or alternate jumping with a friend to get to 100.

5. Run the 100-yard dash.  For younger children, try running 100 feet!

6. Alternate hopping on one foot, then the other, then two feet to get to 100.

7. Play hopscotch by 10s.  Draw a hopscotch board counting by 10s.

8. Try using a hula hoop while counting to 100.

9. Alternate sliding to the left 10 times, then to the right 10 times. Keep going, counting by 10s to 100.

10. Bounce 100 times on a large fitness ball.

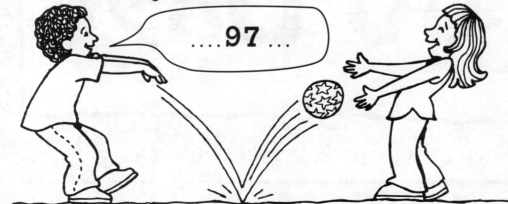

....97 ...

# 100 Footprints Path

## Materials

☐ 100 laminated footprints numbered 1 to 100 (page 10)

☐ tape or adhesive

## Teacher Preparation

A footprint path can be a great way to practice counting and skip counting.  It is also a great way to work a little physical activity into the daily routine. Things to consider:

• Do you want to add a footprint each day and build up to the 100th day, or do you want to set up the 100 Footprints Path all at once?

• Do you want the path in the classroom, in the hallway, or outside?

• Do you want to surprise students and set up the path on the 100th Day leading right to your classroom?  You could start with the first footprint at the front door of the school and lay them down ending with the 100th footprint at the decorated classroom door.

Once you know, use the patterns on page 10 to prepare a colorful footpath.  Make fifty left footprints and fifty right footprints using different-colored construction paper.  Laminate the footprints for greater durability and adhere them to the ground or floor using tape.

## Directions

1. Students can walk on the 100 Footprints Path and call out each number as they go.

2. Students can hop, or tiptoe, while saying the numbers.

3. Students can walk backwards to count, too!

4. After the 100 Days Celebration, try some of the suggested activities to incorporate the 100 Footprints Path into your routine.  Once established, use the path every day.  Try these activities:

   • Walk, hop, or jump to different numbers.

   • Find the 5s.

   • Only step on the even numbers or the odd numbers.

   • Put stickers on the 10s.

# Footprint Patterns

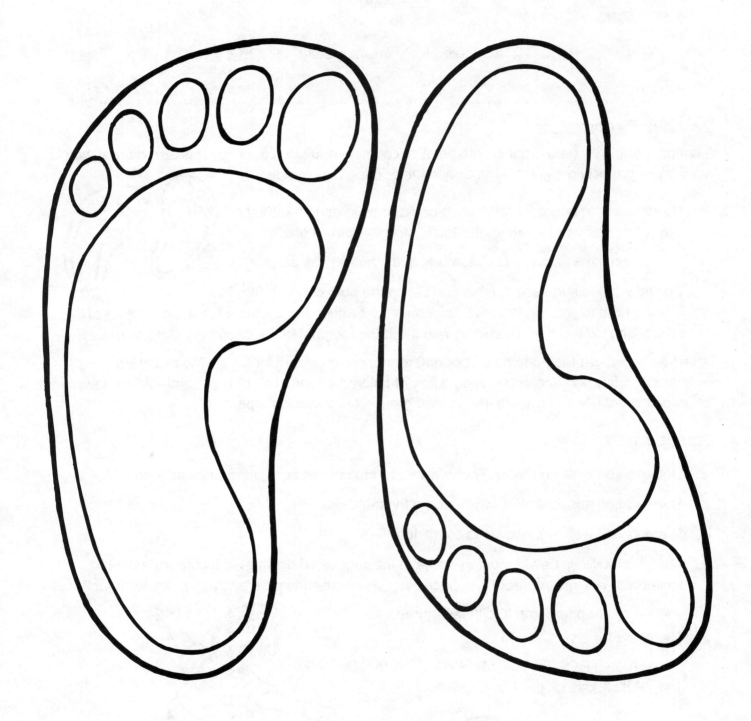

**Left Footprint**                    **Right Footprint**

# Start a Class Memory Book

## Materials

- [ ] construction paper or poster board for the cover
- [ ] 20 pieces of copy paper or lined paper
- [ ] photos
- [ ] markers, pencils, crayons
- [ ] connecting rings

## Assemble a Class Memory Book

1. Make a cover for the *Class Memory Book*. Take a picture of the class and attach it to a piece of construction paper or poster board. Add a title and/or decorations, and laminate the completed cover.

2. Laminate a second piece of heavy paper to use as the back of the book.

3. Add pages between the cover and the back of the book, and use two or three rings to connect the pages. Add additional pages as needed throughout the year.

## Using the Class Memory Book

1. Begin adding to the book by writing a line or two each day highlighting a special activity or topic, or by adding a photo of a special moment. Ask the students: "What did we learn today?" or "What did we do today that was fun?" Explain to students that the *Class Memory Book* will be a journal of sorts.

2. As time progresses, students should become more comfortable suggesting topics or photo opportunities for the class book.

3. Encourage students to take turns writing or drawing in the *Class Memory Book* as writing skills improve.

## On or Before the 100th Day

1. When the 100th day arrives, review these memories and musings. Set aside a time to have a "reading" and allow students to discuss and vote for their favorite experiences to date in school.

2. If you notice a few activities taking most of the votes, add a math activity by creating a chart or tally sheet to vote for the favorite.

3. You may wish to schedule the reading for another day in the week of the 100th Day Celebration to allow for enough time and attention.

4. If you decide to continue this activity to the end of the year, students can later reflect on their favorite activities from the whole year.

# Self Portraits

## Materials

☐ paper, pencils, crayons          ☐ frames for Self Portraits (page 13)

## Directions

**1.** Ask each student to draw his or her self-portrait on or near the first day of school.

**2.** Each student should fill in the blank in the sentence on the frame (e.g. *first, second,* etc.).

**3.** On the 100th day, revisit the activity and have each student do another self-portrait.  This time, add 100th in the blank in the sentence below the portrait.

**4.** In the days following the 100th Day Celebration, provide time for students to compare their two portraits, discuss differences and similarities, and answer the questions below.

My name is _____.

Look at me!

Have I changed in 100 days?          **Yes**          **No**

What is the same in both pictures? _____

How have I changed? _____

_____

_____

Did I add more detail in one of the pictures?          **Yes**          **No**

If so, what did I add? _____

_____

How has my drawing style changed in 100 days? _____

_____

_____

# My Self Portrait

This is my self portrait on the _____ day of school.

# The Reading Tree

### Materials

☐ paper tree handmade or "store-bought"          ☐ paper leaves

## Directions

1. Create and display a special Reading Tree in your room. A simple tree can be fashioned on the wall using crumpled brown paper for the trunk and branches and construction paper for the leaves. You could also use a pre-made tree bulletin board. If you are really creative—create a freestanding tree in the room! This can be fashioned out of chicken wire and covered with paper, or made with cardboard. You will think of many uses for it as the year progresses and the seasons change.

2. Explain to students that each time a book is read, the book's title and the author's name will be written on a leaf. To help keep track, there is also a space on the leaf to write the number to keep a running total of how many books have been read. Fill in each leaf and then add it to the tree. Most likely, students will be paying close attention as the number nears 100!

3. A list of suggested books with the 100-day theme is provided on page 15. If possible, incorporate these books here and there to maintain interest and enthusiasm for the 100th day of school. Read other books as well that relate to your theme or students' interests. Just remember to make a leaf for each book read and add it to the class Reading Tree.

4. Ask students to predict how many books they think will be read by the 100th day. Create a chart or simply keep a list of student predictions near the tree.

5. See how many books were read by the 100th Day. Did you reach your goal? Whose prediction came the closest?

Title: _____

_____

Author: _____

Number: _____

# 100 Days Books

Here is a selection of books to collect or borrow from the library. See how many your class can read.

- ☐ *100th Day Worries* by Margery Cuyler
- ☐ *100 Days of Cool* by Stuart J. Murphy
- ☐ *100 Days of School* by Trudy Harris
- ☐ *100 Hungry Ants* by Elinor J. Pinczes
- ☐ *100 School Days* by Anne Rockwell
- ☐ *Centipede's One Hundred Shoes* by Tony Ross
- ☐ *Counting Our Way to the 100th Day* by Betsy Franco
- ☐ *Curious George Learns to Count from 1 to 100* by H.A. Rey
- ☐ *Emily's First 100 Days of School* by Rosemary Wells
- ☐ *Fancy Nancy: The 100th Day of School* by Jane O'Connor
- ☐ *Fluffy's 100th Day at School* by Kate McMullan
- ☐ *From One to One Hundred* by Teri Sloat
- ☐ *I'll Teach My Dog 100 Words* by Michael Frith
- ☐ *Jake's 100th Day of School* by Lester L. Laminack
- ☐ *Miss Bindergarten Celebrates the 100th Day of Kindergarten* by Joseph Slate
- ☐ *One Hundred Days (Plus One)* by Margaret McNamara
- ☐ *One Hundred Is a Family* by Pam Muñoz Ryan
- ☐ *One Hundred Monsters in My School* by Bonnie Bader
- ☐ *One Watermelon Seed* by Celia Lottridge
- ☐ *The 100th Day* by Grace Maccarone and Alayne Pick
- ☐ *The 100th Day of School* by Angela Shelf Medearis
- ☐ *The 100th Day of School* by Brenda Haugen
- ☐ *The 100th Day of School* by Matt Mitter
- ☐ *The Night Before the 100th Day of School* by Natasha Wing
- ☐ *The Wolf's Chicken Stew* by Keiko Kasza

## MORE BOOKS

- ☐ _____
- ☐ _____
- ☐ _____

# A Sticky Note a Day for 100 Days

## Materials

☐ sticky notes          ☐ markers, pencils, crayons

## Directions

1. At the end of each day, ask students, "What did we learn today? "or "What was the most fun?"

2. As the students respond, write the responses on chart paper. Vote for the favorite choice and write it on a sticky note.

3. Each day, attach the sticky note to a bulletin board or display area. In a pinch, use a large sheet of poster board that can be taken out each day. Place the notes so that eventually they will form the number "100." This can be done directly, or you can "appear" to be placing the notes and pictures randomly. Then, wait and see how long it takes for students to notice the "100" pattern you are making.

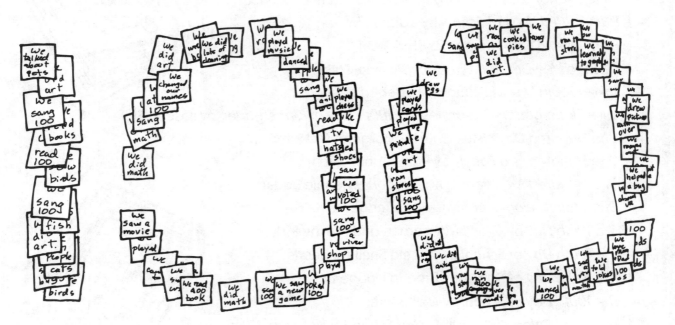

4. When the 100th day arrives, review these memories. Set aside a time to have a "reading" and allow students to discuss and/or vote for their favorite experiences to date in school.

5. If you notice four or five activities taking most of the votes, add a math activity by creating a chart or tally sheet to vote for the favorite. (Note: You may wish to schedule the reading for another day in the week of the 100th Day Celebration to allow for enough time and attention.)

6. If you decide to continue this activity to the end of the year, students can reflect on their favorite activity from the whole year.

# We Can Name 100...

## Materials

- ☐ 12" x 18" colored construction paper
- ☐ 12" x 18" white construction paper
- ☐ felt pens
- ☐ 2" book binder rings

## Teacher Preparation

1. Make a large book using large pieces of construction paper. If your school has a copy machine that can accommodate large pieces of construction paper, number a page 1 to 100 and then copy the page on to construction paper. Then, add a different title to each page.

2. Make a cover that says *We Can Name 100...*

3. Write a different topic heading on each page.
   Here are some possibilities:
   - 100 Animals
   - 100 Places to Visit
   - 100 Things in Nature
   - 100 Nouns
   - 100 Names
   - 100 Verbs
   - 100 Foods (Categorize the food using the five food groups.)

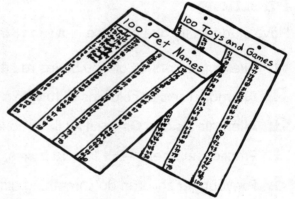

4. Punch holes in the tops of the pages and put them together using binder rings. More pages can be added later.

## Directions

1. Introduce the *We Can Name 100...* book to the students. Prop it up on a wall or easel so that it will be accessible and easy to write on. Explain that it is a special project and one that they will work on from time to time throughout the school year.

2. After students have heard you read the topics, ask them to pick one to start.

3. Work with students to brainstorm as many words as they can think of to add to that topic. Write the words they suggest and explain that they will add to the list as they think of more words.

4. From time to time, take out the book and brainstorm to add to one or more of the lists. This might work best at the end of the day, or as a transitioning activity. If you have a science, social studies, or a language arts-related list, review it during that class period.

5. As the year progresses, invite students to add to these book pages on their own. Periodically review the list and count how many items are listed or how many are still needed.

# 100s Grid Activities

> ## Materials
> ☐ 100s Grid (page 19)
> ☐ crayons, markers, pencils
> ☐ optional: stickers, small buttons, jewels, etc.

## Teacher Preparation

1. Run off copies of the 100s Grid for each student.

2. This activity can be done over time. Try doing a row or two per day until it is completed.
   **Note:** Older students can write the numbers from 1–100 in the boxes to start.

## Directions

Have students try one of these ways to fill in the boxes:

1. Alternate colors—Color 10 boxes red, then 10 boxes blue, then 10 boxes yellow, etc.

2. Alternate rows or columns of 10 with school colors.

3. Alternate **Xs** and **Os**—Put **Xs** in 10 boxes, then put **Os** in 10 boxes and repeat five times.

4. Practice numbers—Put **1s** in 10 boxes, then **2s** 10 boxes, then **3s**, etc.

5. For younger children do something different for each row or column of 10.

Do one row each day. Here are some suggestions for younger children:

○ Put circles in 10 boxes.

☺ Put smiley faces in 10 boxes.

♥ Put hearts in 10 boxes.

☆ Put stars in 10 boxes.

/ Put diagonal lines in 10 boxes.

→ Put an arrow in 10 boxes.

— Put horizontal lines in 10 boxes.

| Put vertical lines in 10 boxes.

▲ Put a triangle in 10 boxes.

✓ Put a check mark in 10 boxes.

*Other ideas:* stickers, buttons, jewels, etc.

# 100s Grid

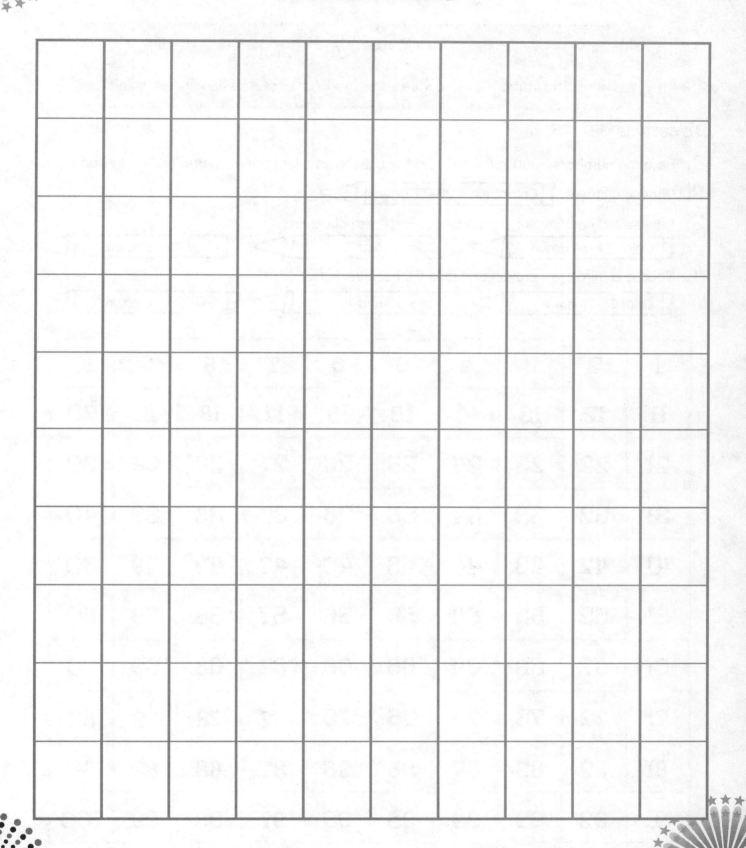

# Mystery Number

## Materials

☐ 100s Grid (page 19)          ☐ crayons, markers, or pencils  (3 different colors)

## Directions

1. Fill in the numbers 1–100 in the 100s Grid or use the smaller pre-numbered grid on this page.

2. Choose a crayon. ▨ Color boxes 22–72 down.

3. Choose a different color crayon and follow these directions:
   ▨ Color 24–74 down.     ▨ Color 25 and 75.     ▨ Color 26–76 down.

4. Choose a third color crayon and follow these directions:
   ▨ Color 28–78 down.     ▨ Color 29 and 79.     ▨ Color 30–80 down.

| 1 | 2 | 3 | 4 | 5 | 6 | 7 | 8 | 9 | 10 |
|---|---|---|---|---|---|---|---|---|----|
| 11 | 12 | 13 | 14 | 15 | 16 | 17 | 18 | 19 | 20 |
| 21 | 22 | 23 | 24 | 25 | 26 | 27 | 28 | 29 | 30 |
| 31 | 32 | 33 | 34 | 35 | 36 | 37 | 38 | 39 | 40 |
| 41 | 42 | 43 | 44 | 45 | 46 | 47 | 48 | 49 | 50 |
| 51 | 52 | 53 | 54 | 55 | 56 | 57 | 58 | 59 | 60 |
| 61 | 62 | 63 | 64 | 65 | 66 | 67 | 68 | 69 | 70 |
| 71 | 72 | 73 | 74 | 75 | 76 | 77 | 78 | 79 | 80 |
| 81 | 82 | 83 | 84 | 85 | 86 | 87 | 88 | 89 | 90 |
| 91 | 92 | 93 | 94 | 95 | 96 | 97 | 98 | 99 | 100 |

# 100s Chart

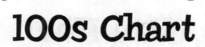

| 1 | 2 | 3 | 4 | 5 | 6 | 7 | 8 | 9 | 10 |
|---|---|---|---|---|---|---|---|---|---|
| 11 | 12 | 13 | 14 | 15 | 16 | 17 | 18 | 19 | 20 |
| 21 | 22 | 23 | 24 | 25 | 26 | 27 | 28 | 29 | 30 |
| 31 | 32 | 33 | 34 | 35 | 36 | 37 | 38 | 39 | 40 |
| 41 | 42 | 43 | 44 | 45 | 46 | 47 | 48 | 49 | 50 |
| 51 | 52 | 53 | 54 | 55 | 56 | 57 | 58 | 59 | 60 |
| 61 | 62 | 63 | 64 | 65 | 66 | 67 | 68 | 69 | 70 |
| 71 | 72 | 73 | 74 | 75 | 76 | 77 | 78 | 79 | 80 |
| 81 | 82 | 83 | 84 | 85 | 86 | 87 | 88 | 89 | 90 |
| 91 | 92 | 93 | 94 | 95 | 96 | 97 | 98 | 99 | 100 |

# Gumball Machine

## Materials

- [ ] 12" x 18" construction paper (variety of colors)
- [ ] gumball machine pattern for each student
- [ ] paint and brushes, stamp pads, or dot stickers
- [ ] paper plate
- [ ] crayons
- [ ] scissors

## Directions

1. Color and cut out the gumball machine pattern below. This will be the bottom of the machine.

2. Glue the pattern to the bottom of the large piece of construction paper.

3. Paint, draw, use fingerprint dots, or add stickers to make 100 gumballs on the paper plate.

4. Glue the paper plate above the pattern to make the top of the gumball machine.

# "Pin the Zero on the 100"

## Materials

☐ 100 mat (page 24)    ☐ zero patterns    ☐ blindfold    ☐ tape

## Teacher Preparation

This game is played like "Pin the Tail on the Donkey."

1. Laminate the 100 mat for durability and attach it to a wall.

2. Use the patterns below to cut out a zero for each student. Put tape behind each zero. It is not nessary to cut out the white centers. Laminate, if possible, so the game can be played again and again.

## Directions

1. Explain to students that they will take turns trying to place a zero where it belongs on the 100 mat. Look at the mat to determine where the missing zero belongs. That will be the target area!

2. Blindfold one student at a time, spin him or her around once (if appropriate), hand him or her a zero with tape on the back, and guide him or her toward the 100 mat on the wall.

## "Pin the Zero on the 100"

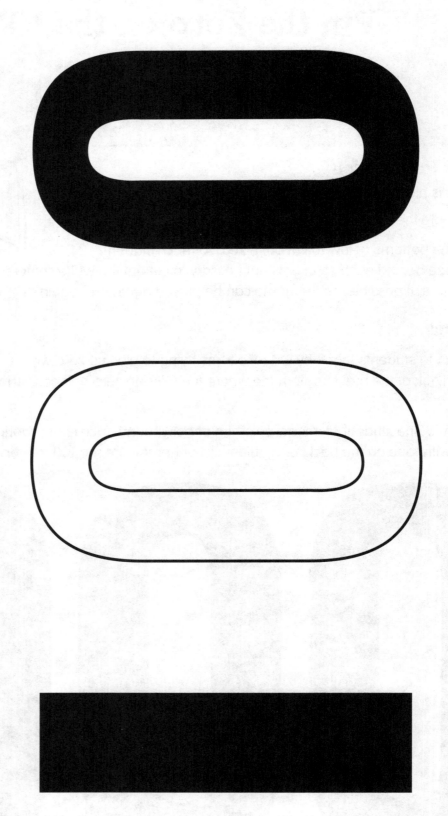

# Counting 10s Fireworks

## Materials

☐ Counting 10s Fireworks page for each student (page 26)

☐ markers or paint          ☐ cotton swabs          ☐ scissors

## Directions

1. Write the number 100 in the center of the Counting 10s Fireworks page.

2. Put 10 dots of color in each of the surrounding sections using markers or by dipping cotton swabs into paint.

3. When the paint is dry, count by 10s to see how many dots were made.

4. Create a "fireworks display" in the classroom using all the finished pages!

5. For extra practice, make copies of this page and have students cut out the cards below. Use the cards for practice counting by tens.

| | | 100 |
|---|---|---|
| 90 | 80 | 70 |
| 60 | 50 | 40 |
| 30 | 20 | 10 |

# Counting 10s Fireworks

# 100 Cubes

## Materials

☐ 100 linking cubes* (at least 100)   ☐ chart paper or poster board   ☐ pens

*If cubes are not available, try interlocking blocks or linking chains.

## Counting the Cubes
## Directions

Ask students, "How long is a line of 100 cubes?" Discuss their ideas and then find out!

1. Have 10 students each put 10 linking cubes together.

2. Ask students to stand shoulder-to-shoulder, each holding their 10 connected cubes.

3. Have the 10 students count off from left to right by 10s to make sure there are 100 cubes. Each student should sit once his or her 10-cube "stick" has been counted.

4. Once all are seated, have the 10 students put their cube "sticks" together.

5. Lay the 100-cube "stick" on the floor. Count to 100 by 10s again.

## Compare and Contrast the Cubes

## Directions

1. Label a chart or graph—*Longer, Shorter,* and *Equal.* Add a title if you wish.

2. Pose the question to students: Are you *longer, shorter,* or *the same size* as the line of cubes?

3. Have students take turns lying down next to the 100 cubes. Observe. Is each student *longer, shorter,* or *equal* to the 100 cubes? Write each name in the appropriate column.

4. Have an adult lie beside the 100-cube "stick" and see if he or she is *longer, shorter,* or *equal to* the 100 cubes.

5. Measure items using the 100-cube "stick." Find items in the classroom that are *longer, shorter,* or *equal* to the 100 linking cubes. Add the names of the items compared to the chart.

6. Divide the cubes into different parts that will equal 100.
   **Examples:** 2 rows of 50, 4 rows of 25, 10 rows of 10.

# 100 Seconds

## Teacher Considerations

1. Determine if you will use props for some of the activities listed below and gather what is needed for the 100 Seconds tests.

2. Decide whether a teacher or another student will hold the timer.

## Directions

Ask students, "What can we do in 100 seconds?" For example, have them close their eyes for 100 seconds and stand up when they think the time is up.
Discuss other ideas for things to do in 100 seconds.

## No Props Needed

1. Be silent for 100 seconds, then yell "100!"

2. Clap your hands for 100 seconds then put your hands behind your back.

3. Stand on tiptoes for 100 seconds.

4. Wiggle in place for 100 seconds.

## Props Needed

1. Read for 100 seconds, then close the book.

2. Toss linking cubes, plastic counters, etc. into a bucket (one at a time) and see who gets the most in 100 seconds.

3. Balance a marshmallow or a pompom on your nose for 100 seconds.

4. Balance a book on your head for 100 seconds.

5. Toss balloons in the air for 100 seconds.

# 100 Inches

## Materials

- ☐ ball of string, yarn, or rope
- ☐ measuring tools
- ☐ rulers
- ☐ scissors

## Teacher Preparation

1. Prepare several 100-inch lengths of string for groups of students. Wrap tape around the ends to prevent fraying.
2. Collect measuring tools such as tape measures, rulers, and yard sticks.

## Directions

1. Ask students to think about different ways to measure and the tools that can be used.
2. Share the measuring tools that have been collected and demonstrate how each might be used.
3. Ask, "How long is 100 inches?" Can students show you with their hands?
4. Have students use the 100-inch lengths of string to measure things in the classroom. Challenge them to find something in the room or the play area that measures exactly 100 inches.

# 100 Feet

## Materials

- ☐ ball of string or rope
- ☐ tape
- ☐ tape measure (100 feet)*
- ☐ rulers

**Note:**
*If 100-foot tape measure is unavailable, measure out 100 feet on a rope or string. Tape the ends.

## Directions

1. Ask students, "How long would 100 feet be?" Can they show you with their hands?
2. Brainstorm answers. Ask for examples at your school. For example, a student response might be "It is 100 feet from our door to the swing set."
3. Outside, or in a hallway, use a tape measure or 100-foot string to measure out how far 100 feet actually is. Then, spend time measuring different areas or things to better understand 100 feet.

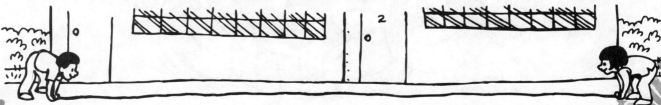

# 100–Link Chains

## Materials

☐ 4" x 6" pad of brightly-colored sticky notes     ☐ rulers     ☐ scissors     ☐ tape measure

## Teacher Preparation

1. Prepare sticky-note strips by cutting the pad up into four, one-inch-wide strips. (Note: 10 pages or so of a sticky-note pad can be cut at a time with a paper cutter or heavy duty scissors.) Each strip will be 6" long. Give each student a small section of the pad, not individual strips.

2. Save enough strips for each student to use one to combine his or her links with another student's links at the end.

## Directions

1. Give each student a section of sticky-note strips to make a paper linking chain.

2. Demonstrate how to use the sticky end of the strip to make the first link. Place the next strip inside the first closed-circle link and close it. Now you should have two connected links.

3. Explain that they will continue to add links until they have short 10-link chains. Then, they will link their 10-link chains together to make longer, 100-link chains.

4. Predict how far a 100-link chain will reach. Will it be 100 inches long? Longer? Will it stretch across the room? If you lay it on the floor, how many children "long" will it be? Will it be longer than a bus?

5. Record the estimates and see who had the best prediction.

6. Decorate the classroom with the 100-link chains.

# 100 Pounds

## Materials

- ☐ different types of scales (at least one that can measure 100 lbs)
- ☐ clear plastic containers
- ☐ 100 items such as teddy bear counters, linking chains, linking cubes, pipe cleaners, chenille sticks, pencils, crayons, or blocks

## Teacher Preparation

1. Gather 100 items of different materials. Ask students to help prepare groups of 100 items by counting out sets of 10.

2. Put the groups of items into clear, similar-sized containers, if possible. If not, explain that to compare, the different items collected will all need to be weighed in the same container.

3. Gather a variety of scales. Demonstrate how to use each scale and how to read each one.

## Directions

1. Ask students to look at the groups of items and determine which they think will weigh the most, and which will weigh the least.

2. Allow time for students to lift the containers, and arrange them in order from lightest to heaviest.

3. Once students have made their decisions, allow time for weighing and comparing.

4. After some practice, introduce the concept of heavier weights and ask, "How much do you think 100 pounds is?" Give students time to discuss their answers. Then, ask, "What might weigh 100 pounds?"

5. Introduce a "bathroom" scale and see what might weigh 100 pounds. Try stacks of books, blocks, a person, a box of paper to be recycled, bricks, etc.

# 100 Ounces

## Directions

### Session 1

1. Ask students, "How much is a liquid ounce?"  Pour an ounce of water into a clear container.

2. Ask students, "How many drops would it take to make an ounce?  More than 100 or less than 100?"  Discuss answers.

3. Mark the ounce level on some measuring cups and give students eyedroppers.  Have students take turns adding 10 drops each until 100 drops have been added to the cups.  Did 100 drops make more or less than one ounce?

### Session 2

1. Ask students,  "What size container would you need to hold 100 ounces?"  Give time to discuss answers and choose containers.

2. Give students cup measures and ask them to measure out 100 ounces.  **Note:** It will take roughly $12\frac{1}{2}$ cups of water to equal 100 ounces.

# 100 Ice Cubes

## Directions

1. Have students count out 100 ice cubes and place them in a large container.  Mark the level.

2. Ask students to estimate how much water will be in the container when the ice cubes melt.  Will it be 100 ounces?

3. Will the level be higher or lower than the 100 cubes?  Use masking tape to mark the levels on the container to show student estimates.

4. Allow the ice cubes to melt and check the results.  Did the level change?  Did it go higher?  Lower?

# Estimating 100

## Materials

☐ 4 (or more) clear jars or clear plastic containers

☐ 100 pennies, buttons, small erasers, balls, toys, pencils, beans, marbles, etc.

**Note:** You will need exactly 100 items for at least one container.

## Teacher Preparation

1. Collect several jars and fill them with different collections of items.

2. Put exactly 100 items in a few of the containers, and don't forget which ones!

## Directions

1. Ask the students to examine the jars and try to determine which jars have exactly 100 items in them.

2. Use tally charts to record their responses.

3. Provide opportunities for students to count the items by first making piles of 10, and then counting by tens.

# 100 Pennies

## Materials

☐ box of 100s of pennies          ☐ note paper          ☐ pencils

## Directions

1. Ask students to estimate how many pennies they think can be picked up with one hand. Could one of them pick up 100 pennies?

2. Write the estimates on the board or a piece of scratch paper and have students take turns picking up handfuls of pennies.

3. Each student should count his or her pennies and compare the results with the estimates.

   **Note:** After reviewing the results, students should realize that it will probably take more than one handful to collect 100 pennies.

4. Challenge students to collect 100 pennies. How might they do it? Work in pairs or groups? Use two hands at once?

5. Have students arrange the pennies gathered in rows or towers of ten until they reach 100!

# Graph 100

## Materials

☐ bar graph for each group or student     ☐ crayons and pencils     ☐ 100 M&M's®

## Directions

1. Ask students, "Can you graph 100 small colorful candies?" Each small group will need 100 candies to start.

2. Ask student groups to sort the candy and make a pile for each color.

3. Next, have students count each color and fill in the correct number of spaces in the correct column of the bar graph.

| Name(s): | | | | | |
|---|---|---|---|---|---|
| | | | | | |
| | | | | | |
| | | | | | |
| | | | | | |
| | | | | | |
| | | | | | |
| | | | | | |
| | | | | | |
| | | | | | |
| | | | | | |
| | | | | | |
| | | | | | |
| | | | | | |
| | | | | | |
| | | | | | |
| | | | | | |
| | | | | | |
| | | | | | |
| | | | | | |
| ○ red | ○ orange | ○ yellow | ○ green | ○ brown | ○ blue |

# 100 Spins

## Materials

☐ brads     ☐ cardstock     ☐ paperclips     ☐ pencils     ☐ spinners (page 36)

## Teacher Preparation

1. Copy the spinner templates onto cardstock.  Laminate if possible.

2. Cut spinners out and place a brad in the middle of each.  Put a paper clip under each brad.

3. Check that the brad is loose enough for the paper clip to spin freely.

4. Show students how to spin the spinner and mark the tally sheet.

## Directions

1. Work in pairs or small groups to spin a spinner 100 times.

2. Take turns spinning a spinner. Try different approaches:  Either take 5 turns each and then switch or switch after each turn and tally mark.

3. Place a tally mark in the correct column on a Tally Sheet for each number landed upon.

4. Which number had the most spins? ☐

| 100 Spins Tally Sheet | | | | |
|:---:|:---:|:---:|:---:|:---:|
| 1 | 2 | 3 | 4 | 5 |
|   |   |   |   |   |

# 100 Spins Spinners

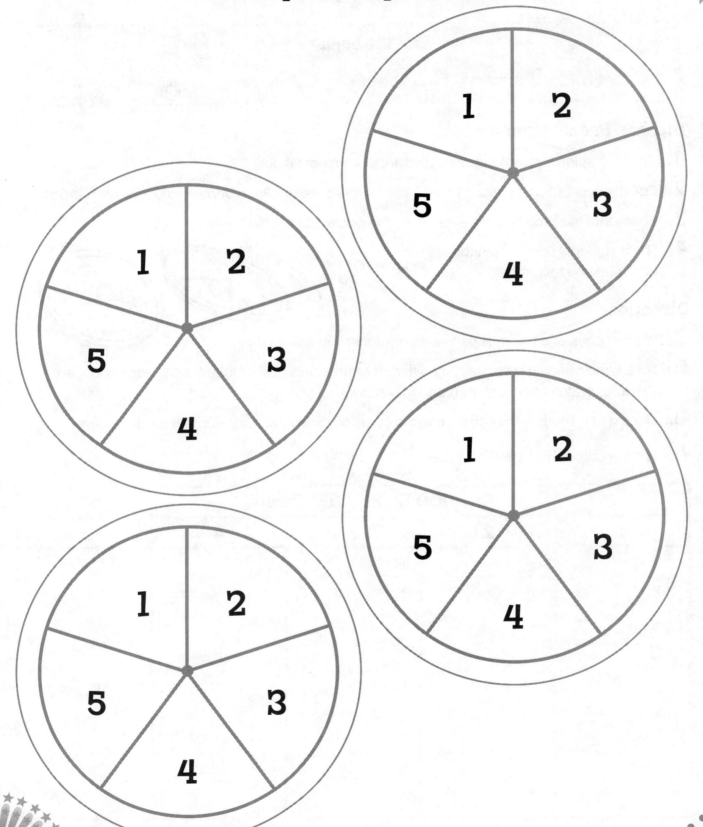

# Flip a Coin — Probability

## Materials

☐ 100s Grid (page 19)      ☐ coins      ☐ pencils and paper

## Directions

1. Flip a coin 100 times. Each time, use the 100s Grid to record whether it landed on heads or tails. Add an **H** or a **T** to keep track.

2. Count the number of **H**s for heads. Count the number of **T**s for tails.

3. Add the number of heads and tails to double-check that the total is 100.

4. Compare the results. Were there more heads flipped or more tails flipped?

# 100 Rolls of the Dice — Probability

## Materials

☐ 100s Grid (page 19)      ☐ dice for each student or group      ☐ pencils and paper

## Directions

1. Roll a die 100 times and record each number rolled on the 100s Grid. This may be done a little at a time.

2. Count the number of times each number was rolled and record the totals on a chart like the one shown here.

3. Compare the results. Discuss.

| 100 Rolls of the Dice | |
|---|---|
| 1 | ⊬⊬  ⊬⊬  ⊬⊬ II |
| 2 | ⊬⊬  ⊬⊬  ⊬⊬ |
| 3 | ⊬⊬  ⊬⊬  ⊬⊬ I |
| 4 | ⊬⊬  ⊬⊬  ⊬⊬ |
| 5 | ⊬⊬  ⊬⊬  ⊬⊬ III |
| 6 | ⊬⊬  ⊬⊬  ⊬⊬ ⊬⊬ |

# The 100s Collections

## Materials
- [ ] 100th Day Collections parent letter (page 39)
- [ ] resealable, plastic sandwich bags for each student

## Teacher Preparation

1. Copy the parent letter for each student to take home.

2. Staple a plastic sandwich bag to each letter.

## Directions

1. Explain to students that they will be bringing the sandwich bag home to their parents with a letter explaining the project. Tell students that each of them will gather and collect 100 items that will fit in the sandwich bag.

2. Spend some time with students estimating what might fit in the bag with students. To start, pose some questions and discuss the answers as a group.

   ? Would 100 live giraffes fit in the sandwich bag? _____ Why not?

   ? Would 100 beads fit in the sandwich bag? _____ Why, or why not?

   ? Would 100 bubbles be a good item to try? _____ Why not?

   ? Could 100 rocks fit in the sandwich bag? _____ Why, or why not?

3. After the discussion, brainstorm a list of things that would be good choices for the snack bag.

## Sharing the Collections

1. The day before the collections are due, remind each student to place his or her collection (in the clear plastic bag) into another bag or container so that no one can see what the collection is. Explain that they want their collections to be surprises.

2. Have students take turns giving clues about their collections to help classmates guess what they are. This activity might take a few days!

3. Display each collection in the classroom after it has been shared and identified. Try different methods of sorting as more collections are added—food items, office supplies, toys, things from nature, man-made things, etc.

4. In the end, depending on what types of items have been brought in, it might be fun to graph the items by collection type.

# 100 Days Collections

Date: _____

Dear Parents/Guardians:

We have been practicing counting and putting items in groups of ten in preparation for our 100s Collections activity. Please help your child put 100 objects in the clear plastic sandwich bag provided. Some examples of things you could put in the bag are given below, but if your child has a better idea, that is great.  Just make sure it isn't alive or edible, and that all 100 items fit in the small, resealable bag!

- 100 beads
- 100 dollar bills (play money)
- 100 erasers
- 100 googly eyes
- 100 paper clips
- 100 pennies
- 100 pebbles
- 100 plastic ants
- 100 pompoms
- 100 stickers
- 100 straws
- 100 squares of paper

## One More Thing!

Each student will have an opportunity to share his or her collection.  They will provide clues and classmates will try to guess what each collection is. (Example:  My collection is soft, and fuzzy, and many different colors—pompoms)  To help with the surprise, please put the small plastic collection bag in another bag that is not see-through.

These wonderful 100s Collection bags are due on _____.

Our 100s Collections will be displayed during our 100th Day Celebration.  We will try to return all the collections, but please do not send items of great value or importance to your family.

Have fun and thank you for your help,

_____

# Brainstorm, Expand, Write

## Directions

**1.** Share the writing prompts below. Have discussions about one or more of them. Older students can choose a prompt to fill in and write about on another sheet of paper.

**2.** If students show interest, consider creating individual books or a class book using the prompts.

**3.** If students are too young to write their own stories, have the class dictate a story based on one of the prompts. For an added challenge, see if the story can be exactly 100 words.

---

If I had $100.00, I would buy_____.

I wish I had 100 _____, because _____.

I can carry 100 _____, but I can't carry 100 _____.

I can do 100 _____, but I can't do 100 _____.

I can see 100 _____, but I can't see 100 _____.

I could eat 100 _____, but I wouldn't eat 100 _____.

100 _____ would fit in our classroom, but 100 _____ would not.

I have _____ 100 times, but I have never _____.

When I am 100, I will _____.

If I had 100 brothers and sisters, I would _____.

---

# Make It with 1 0 0

## Teacher Preparation

1. Cut out the numerals to make 100 for each student or prepare sets of large die-cut numbers.

2. Explain to students that they will be using the three numerals to make a picture.

## Directions

1. Gather all three numerals. Spend some time arranging them in different ways to see what they might make.

2. Glue the numerals on a piece of paper when you know where they will be placed for the picture.

3. Draw a picture incorporating the three numerals. *Examples:* person with glasses, fairy princess with a wand, a vehicle.

4. Write a caption to describe the picture.

- - - - - - - - - - - - - - - - - - - - - - - - - - - - - - - - - - - -

# Find the Words

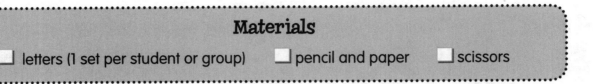

## Materials

☐ letters (1 set per student or group)   ☐ pencil and paper   ☐ scissors

**Teacher Preparation**

1. Copy the set of letters below for each student or group.

d o n e

r e d

**Directions**

1. Ask students to cut out the ten letters and use them to spell *one hundred*. Remind them that the line should be at the bottom on the letters so an *n* is not confused with a *u* or the *d* is not mistaken for a *p*.

2. While they are cutting out the letters, explain that they will be using the letters to spell other words. For instance, you can spell the word *under* using the letters in the word *hundred*.

3. Do a few together and write the words on the board or a tablet.

n o n e

4. Give students time to arrange the letters to try and spell different words.

5. Ask students to call out words as they find them or add to the existing list.

| | | | | |
|---|---|---|---|---|
| o | n | e | h | u |
| n | d | r | e | d |
| o | n | e | h | u |
| n | d | r | e | d |

# 100 Cups

## Materials

- [ ] 100 small Styrofoam, paper, or plastic cups per student or group
- [ ] writing prompt for each student
- [ ] camera

## Teacher Preparation

1. Determine how many students will work on the building project at one time. Will this be a group project or an individual project?

2. Establish an area where students can work that will not be disturbed each day by other activities.

## Directions

1. Count out 100 cups by 2s, 5s, or 10s with students. Ask them what they could build out of 100 cups. Could they make buildings, towers, fences, castles, mountains, etc.? Brainstorm a list of ideas.

2. Have the students take turns building with the cups. Encourage them to stack the cups and arrange them in different patterns or structures.

3. Have the students talk about their structures with partners or in small groups.

4. Ask students to dictate or write about their structures. Start with the following prompt:

    I built a _____ with 100 cups.

5. Take a picture of each structure with the student or group who built it.

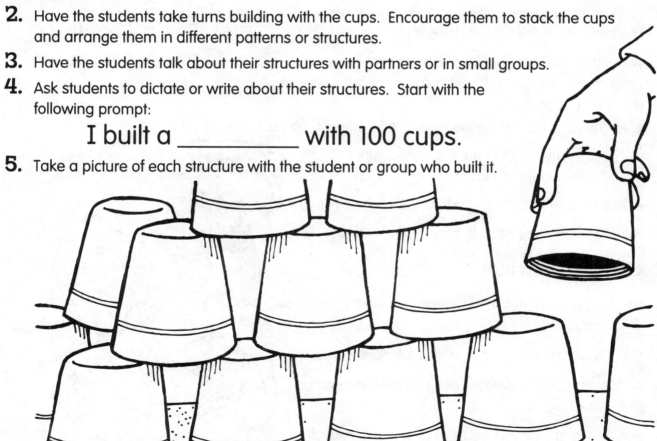

# Name in the Chart

## Materials

☐ 100s Grid (page 19)      ☐ crayons      ☐ pencils

## Directions

1. Show students the 100s Grid. Count the squares by ones or by tens.

2. Ask students how many times they think they can fit their own names into the grid if they put one letter in each box and do not skip any boxes.

3. Ask each student to use a pencil to write his or her estimate at the top of the grid and then start writing his or her name in the boxes.

4. Students should keep writing until all of the boxes are filled. The last name written needs to be a complete name.

5. When the boxes are all filled in, ask students to go back and mark each name. There are a number of ways to do this:

   ✐ Color the box for the beginning letter of each name.

   ✐ Outline the boxes for each name with a different-colored crayon.

   ✐ Alternate two colors to show every other name.

   ✐ Cover the first letter of each name with a sticker.

## MORE Name Activities

1. See how many times the students can write their name in 100 seconds.

2. Get 100 autographs from people at school.

3. Graph or chart the number of times different names fit in the 100s grid.

4. See how many different names fit in the 100s Grid.

# Gift of 100 Cards

## Materials

- ☐ templates for card sentiments (page 46)
- ☐ crayons and markers
- ☐ envelopes
- ☐ paper to make cards

## Teacher Preparation

1. Think about how the one hundred cards will be sent. If they will be sent in bulk in large manila envelopes, the type of fold for the card will not matter.

2. If individual envelopes will be used, more guidance will be needed to design and fold cards.

3. This project can take weeks to complete. You may wish to create a bin or box for completed cards until it is time to send or deliver them.

## Directions

1. Propose making 100 cards for people to make them feel better.

2. Discuss who would enjoy receiving cards. Perhaps soldiers, or people in the hospital would be good. Or perhaps there is a family or group related to the school that would enjoy the gift of cards.

3. Practice folding paper to make the cards. Paper can be folded in half vertically or horizontally, or in quarters.

4. Have students decorate cards and write messages inside, or use the templates provided. This may take a few days or weeks.

5. Periodically count the completed cards as a class. Count by ones or make stacks of five or 10 and count the groups.

6. Once there are one hundred cards they can be delivered. Take the cards to a hospital, senior center, or other group, or mail them to an armed services headquarters.

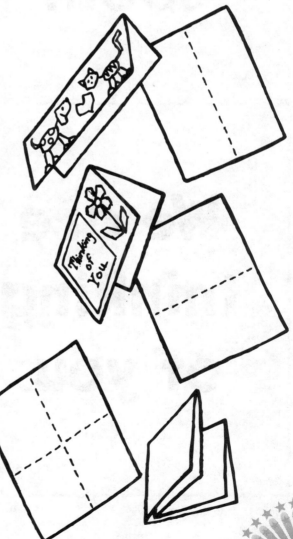

# Gift of 100 Cards (cont.)

| | |
|---|---|
| Hope you feel better soon! | Thinking of you! |
| We are thinking of you. | Thank you for your service! |

# How Do You Say 100?

**Materials**

☐ small sticky notes    ☐ map or globe    ☐ pencil, markers, and scissors

1. How do you say *one hundred* in other languages?

2. If there are children who speak different languages in your class, ask them how to say one hundred in their language. Write each new way on a sticky note.

3. Here are some translations. Others can be found online.

| Chinese | bai |
|---------|-----|
| English | hundred |
| French | cent |
| German | einhundert |
| Greek | ekatón |
| Hebrew | me'a |
| Japanese | hyaku |
| Korean | baek or baeg |
| Polish | sto |
| Portuguese | cem |
| Spanish | ciento |
| Thai | nueng-roi |

4. Make a sticky note for "one hundred" in each different language.

5. Place the sticky notes on a map or globe to show where the different languages are spoken.

 hyaku     sto     ciento     bai

# When I Am 100. . .

## Materials

- ☐ 12" x 18" colored construction paper (a variety of colors)
- ☐ glue
- ☐ head pattern (page 49)
- ☐ markers and colored pencils
- ☐ cotton balls or gray or white yarn
- ☐ optional: eye stickers, jewels, fabric for clothes

## Teacher Preparation

1. Run off copies of the head pattern for each student.

## Directions

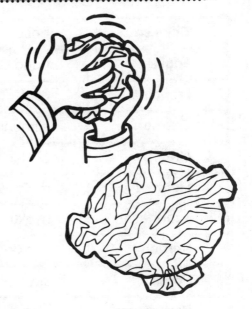

1. Ask students what they think they will look like when they are 100 years old. Discuss the possibilities. Explain that they will be making portraits of themselves as they might look at 100.

2. Have the students cut the head patterns out and crumple them up, flatten them, and ball them up again. Do this a few times to create wrinkles.

3. Glue the wrinkled head pattern onto a piece of colorful construction paper. Leave room above for a name, the hair, and/or hat. Leave room below for clothes.

4. Ask each student to add a nose, eyebrows, and mouth. Either use eye stickers or draw eyes on the face.

5. Think about the hair. Will they have gray or white hair? Will it be long or short, or will they be bald? Use crayons, yarn, or cotton balls for hair, mustaches, or beards.

6. Add eyeglasses if they think they will wear glasses.

**A Little Something Extra**—Use an Aging App. Input the students' pictures in it and it will show what they might look like when they are much older.

# When I Am 100... *(cont.)*

**Head Pattern**

# Life 100 Years Ago

## Materials

☐ poster board            ☐ glue            ☐ writing materials

## Teacher Preparation

**1.** Use the library or the Internet to find interesting facts about life 100 years ago. Try to find information that would be of interest to your students based on where you live. Is it a farm community, a city, or an area near the water?

**2.** Discuss the differences such as the clothing worn, types of transportation, where food came from, and what was studied in school. Download pictures and find books to create a display.

**3.** Think about a time when there was no electricity, no computers, and no cell phones. Consider having a day without electricity. Have students brainstorm a list of things they would miss doing. Then ask them to think of things they could do instead.

**4.** Discuss games that are still played like tag, jacks, jump rope, football, marbles, capture the flag, and chess. What games do we have now that did not exist 100 years ago?

**5.** If possible, invite someone who is 100 years old to come in and talk about what life was like when he or she was the age of your students.

**6.** Discuss what school might be like 100 years from now.

100 Years Ago

Now

# Ten Ideas to Set Up Your Classroom

Decide which of these ideas suit your classroom—and the time you have—and get started! Some ideas can be prepared and displayed in advance, some can be done with students, and some can be surprises for the 100th Day Celebration.

1. Send home the informational parent letter (page 52) and the 100 Days Collections parent letter (page 39).

2. Decorate your classroom door. Hang streamers and a sign with the words: "We're 100 Days Smarter!"

3. Put 100 holiday lights up around the room.

4. Cut out 100 strips of fabric and help students tie the strips to a string to make a "ragamuffin" garland. String the garland in the classroom.

5. Make a poster using the 100 leaves from The Reading Tree activity. (See page 14.)

6. If you have double doors in the school, you can put a zero around each door and a one to the left of the doors to make a giant 100.

7. Cut out a giant heart and have the students put handprints or fingerprints all over it until you have 100 prints. Call it the "100-Prints Heart."

8. Place a road on a bulletin board and place different vehicles that the students have made on the road and title it, "We're On Our Way to the 100th Day!" or you could do the same thing with a train track and title it, "Chugging Along to the 100th Day!"

9. Stretch bulletin board paper all the way across the hall. The number 100 should be drawn on it large enough for a student to walk through the holes cut out of the zeros.

10. Hand out a precut heart to each student. Ask each student to write something they love about their school. Place these hearts on a bulletin board in the shape of 100. The title can be: "100 Reasons Why We Love Our School."

# 100th Day Celebration

Date: _____

Dear Parents/Guardians:

Our class will be having a celebration to commemorate a very special day. *The 100th Day of School Celebration* will be on _____.

We have been working hard to prepare for this exciting day. Much of our work will be displayed. We will share special stories and food treats. Special games and activities are planned as well.

We are looking forward to this day and hope your child can participate to make it even more fun.

We were hoping that each child could _____

_____

_____

Thank you,

_____

# Food Treats for Your Classroom

1. Write numbers 1–100 on 100 pieces of wrapped candy and hide them all over the classroom. As students find the numbered candies, have them color in the numbers on a 100s Chart. (See page 21.)

2. Create a snack treat in a resealable snack bag that looks like the number 100. Use a wafer cookie for the 1 and two round cookies for the zeros. Arrange them in order in the plastic bag and seal.

3. Give each student a pretzel stick and two round crackers to form the number 100.

4. Provide 10 bowls of different small snacks (cereal, shape crackers, jellybeans, grapes, etc.). Give each student a cup or bag. Have students count 10 of each snack and add it to their bags. Count by 10s to reach 100.

5. Bake a cake using two round pans. Cut out the center of each cake to create the zeros. Cut the circles removed to form the number 1. Frost the three pieces, decorate them, and display.

6. Make or buy cupcakes or sugar cookies. Frost them and arrange the treats on a tray in the shape of 100 to share with students.

7. Make or buy cupcakes or sugar cookies. Have each student decorate one with a 100 on top. To make the 100, provide cut pieces of licorice for the number 1 and two circular candies for the zeros.

8. At breakfast, see if the cafeteria can give students one link sausage and two pancakes to form the number 100.

9. Give each student a pack of Smarties® and tell each one of them that he or she is 100 days smarter.

10 Make a goldfish "bowl" out of paper. Put the bowl in a resealable plastic bag and then put 100 goldfish crackers in the bag.

# 100th Day Celebration Activities

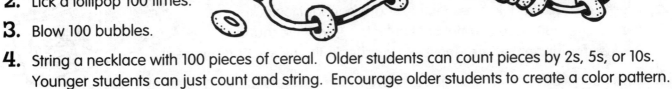

Here are some quick, easy, and affordable ideas that you can do on this day:

1. Work a 100-piece puzzle.

2. Lick a lollipop 100 times.

3. Blow 100 bubbles.

4. String a necklace with 100 pieces of cereal. Older students can count pieces by 2s, 5s, or 10s. Younger students can just count and string. Encourage older students to create a color pattern.

5. Do math word problems that equal 100.
   **Example:** John had 25 gumballs, Ted had 25 candy bars, Aiden had 25 pieces of gum, and Gwen had 25 peppermint candies. How much candy did the four people have in all?

6. Fill in the Happy 100th Day page (on page 57).

7. Cut out 100 1-inch squares for each student to use to make a mosaic.

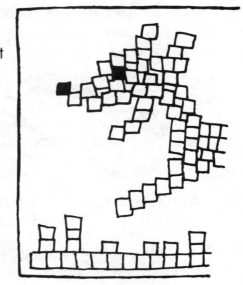

8. Stand 100 dominoes up. Gently push the first one on the count of 3 and watch them fall in sequence.

9. Make a cape or headpiece from a shower curtain or large piece of cloth. Attach one hundred items to it and call the student wearing it the Hundred Hero.

10. Make a tree out of 100 twigs or stick pretzels. Glue them to a piece of paper. Then add leaves to the tree.

11. Practice counting up to 100 or back down from 100.

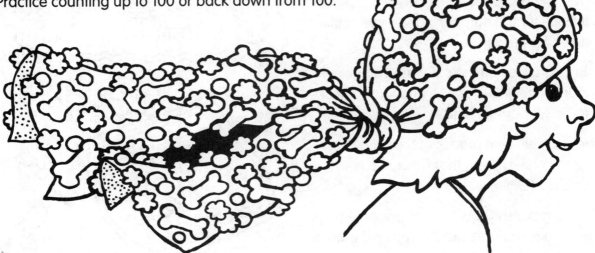

# The 100 Days Hat

There are so many ways to make celebratory hats. Here are a few options to get started.

## Materials

- ☐ baseball cap, visor, or other type of hat (often can be found in craft stores or $ bins)
- ☐ collections of 100 items (buttons, pompoms, bows, etc.)
- ☐ glue

## Directions

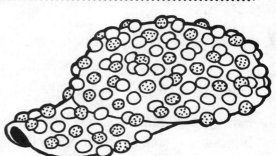

**1.** Have the students count their collections of 100 items.

**2.** Then, have each student glue his or her collection to the hat he or she has chosen.

**3.** Let the hats dry and wear them proudly!

# The 100 Days Crazy Headband

## Materials

- ☐ 10 strips of paper approximately 2" x 10" long (10 strips per child)
- ☐ art supplies such as small stickers, stamp pads and stampers, or paint
- ☐ cotton swabs
- ☐ long strips of heavy paper (2" wide), colorful border trim, or sentence strips (one per child)

## Directions

**1.** Fit a sentence strip, section of border trim, or strip of heavy paper to each student's head but do not staple it closed.

**2.** Put 10 small stickers, 10 stamps, or 10 paint dots on each of the ten strips of paper.

**3.** Have students staple the completed strips to the headband.

**4.** Either let the strips hang out and sway or bring all of them together and staple all 10 together at the top.

**5.** Add "I'm 100 Days Smarter!" labels to each headband. Staple the ends of the strip together to finish the headband.

# We Are 100 Days Smarter!

## Materials

- ☐ enlarged Number Cards 1–100 (pages 58–64)
- ☐ large sheet of bulletin board paper
- ☐ markers and art supplies

## Directions

1. Have students make a banner that says: "We Are 100 Days Smarter!"

2. Line up approximately 100 students (from mulitple classrooms) and give each one of them an enlarged number card to hold.

3. Have the students position themselves in order from 1 to 100. Remaining students can hold the banner and kneel in front of the 100 students holding the number cards.

4. This makes a great photo opportunity. Either keep the students in the 1 to 100 line, or rearrange them in rows to fit in a picture.

5. Call the school photographer or the local newspaper to document the accomplishment.

# Happy 100th Day!

_____ is 100 days smarter.

**100**

The date of the 100th day of school is...

This is me in 100 years.

**100**

I wish I had 100...

Things I've Learned in 100 Days

**100**

**100**

Look what I can do 100 times.

**100** If I had 100 dollars... **100**

**100** **100**

Color all the 100s! **100**

# Number Cards

## Directions

Copy the number cards (pages 58–64), laminate them, and cut them out. These number cards can be used to practice counting or sorting odd and even numbers. Other ideas include enlarging and laminating the cards to be used to count down to the big day or celebrate the big day. (see page 56.)

# Number Cards (cont.)

| 11 | 12 | 13 |
| 14 | 15 | 16 |
| 17 | 18 | 19 |
| 20 | 21 | 22 |
| 23 | 24 | 25 |

# Number Cards (cont.)

| 26 | 27 | 28 |
| 29 | 30 | 31 |
| 32 | 33 | 34 |
| 35 | 36 | 37 |
| 38 | 39 | 40 |

# Number Cards (cont.)

| | | |
|---|---|---|
| 41 | 42 | 43 |
| 44 | 45 | 46 |
| 47 | 48 | 49 |
| 50 | 51 | 52 |
| 53 | 54 | 55 |

# Number Cards (cont.)

| | | |
|---|---|---|
| 56 | 57 | 58 |
| 59 | 60 | 61 |
| 62 | 63 | 64 |
| 65 | 66 | 67 |
| 68 | 69 | 70 |

# Number Cards (cont.)

| 71 | 72 | 73 |
| 74 | 75 | 76 |
| 77 | 78 | 79 |
| 80 | 81 | 82 |
| 83 | 84 | 85 |

63

# Number Cards (cont.)

| | | |
|---|---|---|
| 86 | 87 | 88 |
| 89 | 90 | 91 |
| 92 | 93 | 94 |
| 95 | 96 | 97 |
| 98 | 99 | 100 |